Eva-Mary

Also by Linda McCarriston

Talking Soft Dutch

Eva~Mary

Linda McCarriston

TRIQUARTERLY BOOKS
NORTHWESTERN UNIVERSITY PRESS

Evanston, Illinois

TriQuarterly Books
Northwestern University Press
Evanston, Illinois 60208-4210

Second TriQuarterly Books/Northwestern University Press
printing 1995

Third TriQuarterly Books/Northwestern University Press
printing 1998

Printed in the United States of America

ISBN 0-8101-5008-5

Acknowledgments

Boston Review: "Hotel Nights with My Mother," "The Stardust," "To Judge Faolain, Dead Long Enough: A Summons."

The Georgia Review: "Bad Lay," "Le Coursier de Jeanne D'Arc."

Green Mountains Review: "In Karlsruhe," "Song of the Scullery."

Seneca Review: "Grateful," "Victorian."

TriQuarterly: "Answer," "The Apple Tree," "Billy," "My Father's Laughter," "My Mother's Chair: 1956," "A Thousand Genuflections," "Tippet."

"A Thousand Genuflections" won the Consuelo Ford Award of the Poetry Society of America.

The author wishes to thank the National Endowment for the Arts for two pre-1989 fellowship grants which allowed time and support to complete this manuscript without threat of censorship, and the Vermont Council on the Arts for its support during the same period.

to Marcia Hill

Contents

~

The Apple Tree

for my mother

~

More beautiful now than ever you were
in pale May blossom, or in August,
gravid again—your chained boughs
bearing, your skirts, stiff camouflage
arustle—you stand, past use, past
prettiness in the winter of your winter,
at the brink of encroaching woods, in the yard
of the old farm, where now, out windows,
curtains shake themselves like rags
from a lost cleaning morning. Here,
in the light that by noon takes
your shadow and carries it from the garden
to the barn, now, from your deep
seeking source under snow, drink long,
breathe slow, be still, as did the child,
she of the single body. The many that
found you and took you are fallen away.

To Judge Faolain, Dead Long Enough: A Summons

~

Your Honor, when my mother stood
before you, with her routine
domestic plea, after weeks
of waiting for speech to return
to her body, with her homemade
forties hairdo, her face purple still
under pancake, her jaw off just a little,
her *holy of holies* healing,
her breasts wrung, her heart
the bursting heart of someone
snagged among rocks deep
in a sharkpool—no, not "someone,"

but a woman there, snagged
with her babies, *by* them,
in one of hope's pedestrian
brutal turns—when, in the tones
of parlors overlooking the harbor,
you admonished that, for the sake
of the family, the wife
must take the husband back to her bed,
what you willed not to see before you
was a woman risen clean to the surface,
a woman who, with one arm flailing,
held up with the other her actual

burdens of flesh. When you clamped
to her leg the chain of *justice*,
you ferried us back down to *the law*,
the black ice eye, the maw, the mako
that circles the kitchen table nightly.
What did you make of the words
she told you, not to have heard her,
not to have seen her there? Almost-
forgiveable ignorance, you were not
the fist, the boot, or the blade,
but the jaded, corrective ear and eye
at the limits of her world. Now

I will you to see her as she was, to ride
your own words back into light: I call
your spirit home again, divesting you
of robe and bench, the fine white hand
and half-lit Irish eye. Tonight, put on
a body in the trailer down the road
where your father, when he can't
get it up, makes love to your mother
with a rifle. Let your name be
Eva-Mary. Let your hour of birth
be dawn. Let your life be long
and common, and your flesh endure.

Billy

~

As though a bare bulb hung
over your head as it does in
movie scenes of interrogation,
you are the single vivid thing
in the shades-of-gray memory,
the white center, out from which
the whole dank tenement
cellar—the dirt floor, the boulders
that formed the old foundation,
the three fat coal-burning
furnaces, one for each of the three
stories, the coal bins punky
across from each, the mud-thick
little windows above that were
coal shutes when the truck came,
the new table-saw, the new
table-saw overhead worklight,
and even our father,
who stood beating you with his fists
where he'd stuck you into
a barrel, as a mountaineer might plant
a banner into a peak, to keep your
skinny thirteen-year-old self erect
till he was finished—the whole
rest emanates and fades.
It was winter. You had driven
your homemade go-cart into a door

that he was saving for something,
I can see the little v's you made
in the paint. I see his upper body
plunging up and down like one
of those wind-driven lawn ornaments,
the one that is pumping.
The barrel reaches your bottom.
You must be holding onto it.
It must be braced against
his table saw. There are no words.
The barrel bangs and scrapes.
Your body sounds different than
a mattress. The noises he makes
are the noises of a man trying to
lift a Buick off the body of
a loved child, whose face he can
see, upturned, just above the wheel
that rests on her chest, her eyes right
on his eyes, as yours were on mine.

A Castle in Lynn

~

In the hometown tonight,
in the quiet before sleep,
a man strokes himself in the darkened
theater of memory. Best old

remembrance, he gets to play it
as slow as he needs, as his hand,
savvy tart of a million reruns,
plays the tune, plays the parts:

now hand is the hard bottom
of the girl. Now hand is full
of the full new breast. Now hand
—square hand, cruel as a spade—

splits the green girlwood of her body.
No one can take this from him now
ever, though she is for years a mother
and worn, and he is too old

to force any again. His cap hangs
on a peg by the door—plaid wool
of an elderly workingman's park-bench
decline. *I got there before*

the boys did, he knows, hearing
back to her pleading, back to her

sobbing, to his own voice-over
like his body over hers: laughter,

mocking, the elemental voice
of the cock, unhearted, in its own
quarter. *A man is king in his own
castle,* he can still say, having got

what he wanted: in a lifetime
of used ones, second-hand, one girl
he could spill like a shot of whiskey,
the whore only he could call *daughter.*

My Mother's Chair: 1956

~

One foot tucked under like a nesting
bird, night after night she sat
in the platform rocker, her eyes
on something I could not see
—her black, Indian, Scorpio eyes—
on no object in the air of the
material room. She rocked
like a man rowing his loved children
out of harm's way, out of the path
of the ocean tanker that bore down
on them out of the fog where he'd
drifted by mistake in the little
loving rowboat of his life. With the
muscles of her arms she rowed
she rocked in that chair going
nowhere, getting out of nothing's
way with the muscles of her thighs, with
her jaw, with her shoulders. From
the kitchen I could watch her be
a piston staying put in the stanchion
of her life with the muscles of her back,
with her hands clamped on the arms
of the rocker as though by strength
she could turn it to a wheel—
and steer—or the reins to a wagon
that she might take up and slap on the backs
of the horses. As a child beats a stick

on the cage of an animal, so a certain
world was playing on her soul.
I stood out of sight who was too
small to leave behind who was too big
to carry. With the muscles of her neck
with the muscles of her chest she plunged
against the leg-trap that must have been
under her. The black telephone,
exquisite as a photo postcard on its
own small table, could listen to her rocket,
could hear the chair threaten to soar.
She never lifted the receiver.
She never asked the black wire to take her
where it could, having already travelled
—a pilgrim, on foot—to that priest,
to that judge, to that doctor.

Good Night, Irene

~

Whose wake was it, whose wedding,
that ended with all of them
singing it in the kitchen, that
thicket of ankles and shins through which
I threaded my way: cuffed gabardines
and brogues, silk hose with the seams
exhausted, the many aunts' Minnie Mouse
pumps? Across the wet floor of the
room—a human supersaturated
solution of rye—to the dutch door
of the pantry that served as the bar,
I rang like a clapper in the bell
of their singing, saw their voices
shimmer together in the well of smoke
that was air. Now I remember—the casket
framed by the drapes of the parlor window,
that room I was too young to enter,
and remember Aunt Peg and Jim
and Chris, Chet and the rest of them
shitface to a man, propped vertical
and rocking with the *I'll see you
in my dreams*. Deep in my animal heart
I took that smell in as a blessing,
that thick smoke of voices as the song.
From behind the shelved half-door
that held the bottles, the butts,
and the feather boas, somebody

lifted me up to see them as who
I was. And I loved them, and hollered
the song, breathing the air of happiness.

Grateful

to my brother

~

I

In the village, when the news broke

—of the two sixth-grade girls, ambushed
in the woods on their way home from school,
raped, tortured, the one surviving
staggering naked onto the tracks so bloody
the trainmen thought the head-to-toe red
was a garment—
    a local friend, by way of
explanation, spilled a couple of local wisecracks:
What makes a woman beautiful? he said. *Jelly doughnuts
and incest.* The boys had been named

who'd dragged the mattresses to the woods,
the guns, the dirty magazines, the axes,
and waited. The whole town knew those boys.
The whole town knew the families
in which those boys were learning this was
sex, the one, in which—the whole town
knew—the son practiced on his sister,

with his Dad. And that silent
little girl? I know what she thought, day,

22

night: another thing to get used to,
growing up.

II

Once, as a child, in an iron lung of dread
the long years of your absence, I told
the priest in confession, the priest Father Welch,
who came to watch the Sox and drink iced tea.
He told me to mind my father.

To obey.

So I put my soul to bed by itself,
so far away that as a woman I still can't
find it, and waited to grow up, to be
a person in the Great World, where men
would be as safe to know as dogs. But, brother,

each line and verse I learned augmented
those seeds of dread, to one Great Wood,
to interlocking branches. Though I often
prayed for you to come home and save me,

looking back I'm grateful
for what kept you away from *the game the whole
family can play*. Robed, studying to be
a priest, you were learning, in books illumined
in gold, the statutes of the overarching code: what,

in other words, we both were spared
your learning at our father's knee. On me.

Hotel Nights with My Mother

~

The hometown flophouse
was what she could afford
the nights he came after us
with a knife. I'd grab my books,
already dreading the next day's
explanations of homework undone
—*I ran out of paper*—the lies
I'd invent standing in front of
the nuns in the clothes I'd lain in
full-bladdered all night, a flimsy
chair-braced door between us
and the hallway's impersonal riot.

Years later, then, in the next
city, standing before my first class,
I scanned the rows of faces,
their cumulative skill in the
brilliant adolescent dances
of self-presentation, of hiding.
New teacher, looking young, seeming
gullible, I know, I let them
give me any excuse and took it.
I was watching them all

for the dark-circled eyes,
yesterday's crumpled costume, the marks
—the sorrowful coloring of marks—

the cuticles flaming and torn.
I made of myself each day a chink
a few might pass through unscathed.

My Father's Laughter

~

When the old fracture
aches in my spine
after waitressing, after
mucking out stalls,

when the changed bone
throbs—a transmitter—
I hear my father's laugh,
a hearty Irish laugh,

laughter that might
have been put to good
use, might have been
one of those loving

father-laughs that men
make over their
daughters, say, when
the daughter drops the ball.

The ball in my back
sticks out to the naked
eye, is a fist when I lie
on the cool floor, a stone

between me and the wood.
It is the place I hang from,

like the woman on the hook
in the Wax Dungeon of

Madame Tussaud: at the
pubis it enters her belly
and emerges in the nave of
her ribcage. From it

she dangles supine, her eyes
in yours, alive in that
instant. Hourly in my body
it is that spot that hooks me

to the past, that pain
that looses my father's
laughter, my father whose
laughter you loved in the

ginmills—he
brought me along. I sat
there, remember?—
my father who when he

took his daughter home
would kick her in his
wingtips—she was
nine and naughty—

around the floor until
her eyes closed. So I do not
recall how that part of
those beatings ended,

but I remember curling
up as a dog would, cornered
by such a man, thinking it
through with that part

of my nine-year-old
mind that thought like
a dog and gave him
my spine.

October 1913

for my father, William

~

In the story it is Philadelphia,
two years since they fled Dromore,
the fire and oil of Presbyterian/Catholic
Ulster near Civil War, of Scottish
and Irish, whole families *turning coat*,
as they say, of Patrick, your father,
and Margaret, your mother, who was
to become a scrapper on the streets
of Lynn, fighting, fist-fighting, the men,
getting knocked to the roadside by
the bosses as she battled for her shoe-factory
union. And what she could not get with her fists
—a big woman, beautiful and vain, crazy
when she drank, often displaying her beautiful
breasts—she got by taking them home,
the men, the way women properly did
to get what they needed.

But in Philadelphia still, it was John.
He came into the kitchen, where you
were the new, fifth baby, the first since him
who was to have been the end, and crying.
It was America, and she could see from the window
a road—not *this* road or *that* road, or road
to here or road to there, but *road*,

way, path, for the first time. Her milk
was still coming in. Her breasts were swollen
and throbbing. It was your fifth day of living,
unnamed, who was to become the minder of fire
in boilers bigger than public buildings
—stories high—crisscrossed
with catwalks of waffled metal, the thick
steel faces roaring your whole shift long
like a bank of hurricanes, the gauges leaping
and trembling toward red, and in each face
a single dense glass lens where the flame stroked
and pried like a living finger. Was she drunk?
Was she raging? Or did she press you
to her shoulder where she stood at the cookstove

lifting the lids off the firebox
with the other hand? Common measures
she had carried in her heart in steerage
aboard the SS Parisian, brutal tools
accustomed to safe-keeping there. One,
two, the crosspiece between, and the whole
rectangle glowed open below you
as John your brother came in,
John the child, with already the child
lost to knowing. She was about
to solve a problem as problems had been solved
crossing back and forth in flight over
the Channel. She was about to undo you,

the way she'd undone a religion
in order to live, the way she'd undone a home
and a country, a name, and a table of faces

lined up where there was no food. Seeing him

see her, she stopped. She crushed the flames
back under the black lids. She would have
nursed you then. She would have sat down
to do it, unbuttoning the bodice on her
scalding breasts. We do not know if,
as she nursed you, she wept.

She wept.

Not Comedy, Not Farce

~

The best we could do was laugh,
and we did, sheer slapstick
in his absence till the tears
we never shed for rage or grief
came down, crumbling our masks
in the pure theater of kitchen:

underpants on heads, costumes
of skillets or silverware, up
on the table or under it, we did
what they must have done out back
of their shanties, in firelight,
far from the Big House—

we danced, we mocked, we cast
our selves to the walls
as shadows big enough to face
a man made of too many lies.
In a morsel of safety you can
make of even the most brutal
tyrant a fool. In the presence
of even one other, a heart-stopping,

lawful terror makes a common
wound of all wounds, makes of all
cringings a shared wordless shame
as sure to bind as love. Music

on the radio, pillows stuffed under
our shirts to trump up the bullying

belly, we swagger-strutted, stumbled
over colors in the linoleum, un-
zipped our flies and watered them
wet, let his broken glasses dangle
like a monkey, off one ear, till our
sides hurt and we held them as we

never dared hold each other.
Long before he set foot on
the boot-camp-scoured front stairs,
sounding like a one-man barroom brawl
hauled up in a wooden wagon, we'd
finished our tea, pulled the plug

on the radio, put the dried cups
back in the closet, the pillows
under our heads, the knives and skillets
under our pillows—everything about us
gone back into dark and quiet, as if
none of it, or us, had eyes or ears.

Girl from Lynn Bathes Horse!!

~

1100 pounds, more or less, the mare
high-steps a trot on a short circle
—two feet of line from the hand
of the Tenement Kid who never outgrew
the wish to be able to do this
to the head of the horse who never
watched TV, never saw The Lone Ranger
or Hoppy, never read about Smoky or
Flicka, Black Beauty or King of the Wind,
and so cannot possibly know that the only
thing the two of them need to perform
this difficult, dangerous act together

is *love*, the kind between cowgirl and pony,
infused as the Garden's knowing. To hell
with experience, instruction, example,
coin of the grownup world. You don't
really need what you don't really own.

In her off hand the stiff hose kinks,
coiling underfoot as the mare circles,
hating the green snake, the water that spurts,
urging her faster, crosser at every turn,
in the tight well of mud, in the slick-
footing'd flood of the yard. *It's a lot like
washing a car*, she quips, as a shod hoof
flies out when the wet slaps horse privates—

It's always like something else, this life

for which squirting a half-ton of horse-in-hand
on the strength of a nine-year-old's metaphysics
is a figure for all the rest, for the morning
by morning invention of a self
in the laboratory of unmarked chemicals.

Childhood is the barrel they give you
to go over the falls in. Whatever you get to take
with you in it can't be bigger or sharper
than an idea. It must be that fall, clenched
in a kid's fist (as earth expresses a diamond),
that transforms it from simply Some Dumb Thing
to Some Dumb Thing that is magic,
the *fifth essence*, perhaps, what the alchemists
knew lay latent in every thing. Even the least.
Even the most ridiculous.

Judgmental

Le vin dissipe la tristesse

~

Years since we first raised glasses
in Alsace, taking our toast from
the cold *krug*, tonight, on the phone,
your voice is a bag of groceries
dropped onto concrete: the slick
unspecific ooze, the glass, the threatened
utter crumble at a touch, at a move.
I'm a bad friend, I'm to understand,
from the sounds you send up as if
from the floor of the ocean, vowels
pitching and yawing in currents
of booze, insistent that I come fetch you.

Though we once thought it funny
to bring up the rear of any three-legged race
together, though we once made a cake
of our special pain and asked nobody else
to the party, though we once kept our
precious otherness like a pet not meant
for the city—a python thick as a thigh,
alive in the room with the Steinway—

friend, from the start, you
were old enough to have played the part
of the mother. But I knew that part,

so I sat you. Nights enough. Enough
the fifths of vodka, the savage,
imperious eye. Now mine is the terror
of the night skater as the etched glass gives,
pitching her down. Mine is the fury
of the one who thrashes airward as ice
hurries, like dread, to mend. And yours,
—God damn me if it must be so—is the face
I know as refuse-to-move, the face graven
on the weight of stone, from which
I will kick, as direction.

The Stardust

~

18 with our fake ID's we started
hitting the nightspots on Route 1,
dives that are structural to strips

like it anywhere. Half-circle
banquettes—fake velvet, fake leather—
tables the size of the barstools,

the joints packed us in, kids
hungry for the smoky dark mapped out
by a handful of patio candles.

We drank exotic blends—sidecars,
grasshoppers—young women, young
men learning to sit the long hours

on cigarettes, on gin, nothing much
in our stomachs, nothing much to say.
Today on the radio I hear the minor

key *plink* of a xylophone, notes
like a Friday night bar, mixed
with guitar and piano. And a simple

grief comes over me like a drink
for what of ourselves we brought
to those holes, willing to be

adults however it was played:
no boredom too great, no darkness too small,
no drug too strong or too often.

Dusk

~

Who first saw in houselights
a haven? Bare road, bare
trees isolate the trailers,
cottages in which the kitchen

is the first to shine come dusk.
It is in houses that women pay
for being women, that children
are winnowed, wheat from chaff.

In a lighted window, I see no
invitation. I see the face of
a woman in an armlock before her
bedroom door, her look a

cadaver's, saying *go outside
and play I'll be ok.* I see
a child whose body, like a
heavy rag, jerks over the

linoleum—a sullen mopping
up of something ugly that
happened. In the boughs outside
the windows shadows gather over

this hour. Some, pillar-like,
form judges, gowned and learned.

Some shape thick bodies of cops
and other fellow elbow-benders.

Priests preside, and the lithe
shapes of lovers the child has yet
to pleasure. Her husband-to-be
is among them. Her unborn sons.

In the dark, a castle is
materializing, and a man.

A Thousand Genuflections

Winter mornings when I call her,
out of falling snow she trots
into view, her tail and mane
made flame by movement, carrying,
as line and motion, back into air
her shape and substance—like fire
into heat into light, turns
the candle takes, burning.
And her head—her senses,
every one is a scout sent out
ahead of her, behind, beside:
her eye upon me, over the distance,
her ear, its million listeners,
delicate and vast her nose, her mouth,
her voice upon me, closing the distance.
I could just put the buckets down
and go, but I kneel to hold them
as she eats, as she drinks, to be
this close. For something of myself
lives here, stripped of the knowing
that is not knowing, a single thing
from the least webbed tissues
of the heart straight out to the tips
of the guardhairs that shimmer off
beyond my sight into air, the grasses,
grain, the water, light.
I've come like this each day

for years across the hard winters,
seeing a figure for the thing itself,
divine—appetite and breath,
flesh and attention. This morning
her presence asks of me: *And might*
you be your body? Might we be
not the figure, but the thing itself?

Victorian

~

At seventy my mother discovers *the orgasm*
in a dream, with someone she cannot remember,
someone not my father, and not the boy who spoiled her
for him when she was a girl—the one he rubbed
her nose in like a reason fifty years of nights
from which days wrapping meat at the Elm Farm
were the respite—someone not the one man, maybe two,
that in her wedded separations, optimist undaunted,
she Let. Imagine. Two live births, the lost ones
between, the men *sawing wood*, the pessaries,
violations routine as the news. Hysterectomy.

No wonder it took a noncorporeal to slip
up under her as she lay, open as a rose in her old
woman's sleep, the bedroom white and blossomy
as a bride's and far from my father's. I wanted
to ask her why she sought down her list of men
for the one who had touched her. I wanted to say:
might it not have been a gift brought warm from
the distaff side, from the one who had loved you since
before you were born and who grieved for the two of you still
that of all the body's possibilities, the one
she had to be sure you learned was to endure?

Tippet

For better than a week
they've dragged it around among
the three houses: the five dogs
I walk with; the diminishing
carcass of a deer. My two
are the old ones, who don't
go off without me, who can't be
running deer, so I look the other way
till my red setter, Kate, *grande
dame* bird-dog, knobby with arthritis,
presents what's left to the front lawn
framed by the big bay window.
No more denying.
So I plow out through a foot of snow
to collar her, queen of the hearth's
circle, gnawing away at the delicate
face of a doe, the balance
of which is a tippet of gray-
gold fur and a strand of flesh
—or a tendon—to the left foreleg
from the knee down, the hoof
a glossy miniature, snowpacked,
hard-packed from its running.
Because I want them not to get
even late a lust for the taste of it,
I head for the covered rubbish
with the creature in my arms, cradling

its skull and bundle of frozen hide,
without thinking, against my breast
like a pet or a child. It hardly
seems grotesque as I do it
to shift it up to my shoulder
—just so—freeing one hand
to lift the lid and slip it in.
I surprise myself, starting to cry then,
having no grave in the iron earth,
no word to lessen the waste
as I throw her away. For solace
I turn to my ignorance—human,
encyclopedic—and say
a shared animal wisdom beyond me
governed this chase. But my flesh
where her head rested
keeps faith with its rue.

Margaret

~

At table fifteen, in the corner,
backlit by a windowful of yellow
almost-autumn and swathed
in shifting smoke that dims
to ritual, to magic, the ordinary
office of the meal, an old
Irishwoman finishes her dinner
with the richest dessert, a fourth
drink, a last cigarette in her hand,

and flashes back at me, enlarged,
my look, which I thought discreet,
as if knowing how deep she enters me.
Is it only that I envy her these
pleasures at her age, a lifetime
undaunted in taking them? Or is it
that in her face, its pasty
monotone, its craggy moonscape
of ruin, I see the blighted,
familiar gene: the habit of soul
that reaches for riot nimbly
as tipping its cap? At the door

she hoists a shawl about shoulders
stout as a man's, shrugs it up
like a man, and arranges her jaw
to a taunt that she turns and tosses

to me, a gesture no longer mine. Were you
the grandmother I cannot remember,

whose eyes were the gauntlet thrown
down, whose eyes were gray ice
sealing wells of sorrow, who would
you come here to find? The woman
cast to be like you, off the template
of your son? Or this failure,
whose very blood I have taken
to be the dare?

Dismantling the Castle

~

May all of your children be writers,
or makers of movies, or sculptors
who will caste you in bronze forever
and stand you in the village square,
your hand lifted into the generations
in a characteristic gesture of love or
destruction from afternoons you may forget,
your feet in their heavy shoes walking
your daughter up the hill at dusk,
or kicking her, the hands of the clock
at six, across the linoleum.
May their words put your words back into
your mouth, verbatim, precise as how
animals learn—crystalline memory:
cowed once, forever cowed—the mare
who will never be touched at the ear
where the first year the twitch
was twisted. May they write your stories
for you, as you told them to their flesh,
make vivid on the page or on the screen
or raise on pedestals of stone, framed
by a city's green, what has passed
as the castle, body to body, in private:
the unforgettable sound of a man's
fist stopping the breath of a child,
the muzzled crying a small body makes
pinned in a grown man's bed, the arc the foot

or the hand cuts in domestic air. And the mouth
carved writing—for the life of the granite—
in the ugliest curse a man can imagine
as he spits it on his little girl,
public—biography—once and for all.

Answer

~

I am the woman you saw, Louise
Bogan, hanging clothes on the line
from the cold back porch
of her tenement, the woman you said
you'd trade to be—free as she seemed
from where you stood at your barred
asylum window. But did your whole
mind ache to be out, to be only
whole enough that day to sort whites
from darks, to man the wringer,
to be that mechanical thing not singing
as she chapped her pale hands raw
in the city wind? Today I went
through the motions that woman
knew, motions I'd guessed
you'd spent your life refusing,
a waking day when my body or my mind
—I can't tell which—dragged
the other from room to room, wiping
fingerprints, washing the bowl,
polishing faucets. It is all I did.
How many have they been, the days like this
when at the end I could stop and thank God watch
the sun finally falling and say again
I didn't give in. I got up and
stayed up and the wash got done and I moved
a whole day closer to the end. Yours

are the poems I want to write but I can't
lie down and be cared for, can't ever crack,
and I hate her, the thick char who
will not fall, that deadweight peasant
who can't be plowed over, plowed under
to crumble and turn in the earth
of her pain into something that flowers.
I believed it when I read it,
but now I don't believe you ever meant
to be her, mere her, mere me, you proud
raku vase whose self preferred to shatter
time and again than to plod
the slack back porches and call it *alive*.

Healing the Mare

~

Just days after the vet came,
after the steroids that took
the fire out of the festering
sores—out of the flesh that in
the heat took the stings too
seriously and swelled into great
welts, wore thin and wept, calling
more loudly out to the green-
headed flies—I bathe you
and see your coat returning,
your deep force surfacing in a
new layer of hide: black wax
alive against weather and flies.

But this morning, misshapen
still, you look like an effigy,
something rudely made, something
made to be buffeted, or like
an old comforter—are they both
one in the end? So both a child

and a mother, with my sponge and
my bucket, I come to anoint, to
anneal the still weeping, to croon
to you *baby poor baby* for the sake
of the song, to polish you up,
for the sake of the touch, to a shine.

As I soothe you I surprise wounds
of my own this long time unmothered.
As you stand, scathed and scabbed,
with your head up, I swab. As you
press, I lean into my own loving
touch, for which no wound
is too ugly.

Lilacs

~

We take our argument out
to the yard, where the children
won't have to listen. Summer
is on us—one of those summer
days that makes you wonder why
you wanted July in the first place,
its weight and heat and stillness
on your body like an extra
fifty pounds. Under the overgrown
lilac, its delicate lavender cones
gone brown, its delicate heart-green
leaves coarsened to dusty leather,
we speak from those places
in ourselves that no one will ever
enter—stones found by ourselves
on the beaches of ourselves,
the tokens we credit with getting us
this far. The two of us, like
the two of them, and them, have not
been able to do it, have not made
the single flawless thing, the one
tool the world wants right for every job.
Who wanted marriage in the first place?
Who wanted the lilacs, the kids,
the house we go outside of to fight?
Don't go yet, I say as you turn,
and you don't, both of us stuck

and wordless in the broth of the air.
What do we look like then as we touch,
as we want to hold each other, and move,
and do? Not the new porch roof
we admire together, its seam invisible
where it meets the old. Not even
the plates you mend, crockery
landscapes glued at a new horizon.
We must look like a man and a woman
loving each other on a stone step,
framed by the darkness of a door
and a grand pair of lilacs.
The gaps between us close a little
as we turn, our arms around each other,
and enter the cool interior.

Joint Custody

One white morning, the near world
fallen all-at-once into winter,
each line to the least twig casting
its negative back, the two

stars of the mares, white on their
bay faces, waver across the white
to me, abreast like twins in the
night sky: Gemini—the son

I called to light under that star,
the boy, ambivalent, who lives
now with his father, now with me.
He is not here, and his absence

is the whole world gone empty-
white, and what is worse, his
absence is to his own heart his own
halving, who thinks of himself

not as we do, his father and me—
light for our dark—but as a
boy who lived whole in his own sky,
even as the earth moved, moves.

In Karlsruhe

for my son

~

In fact, your terrors scared me—
the goat you saw in the mirror
of our Army apartment, the eyes
you described so clearly, slits
widening in your room in the dark
after I'd tucked you in and almost-
closed the door. The woman who then
charged, theatrically potent, in

to slam the dressing-table doors
shut with a bang, to chase with a broom
from under your bed and behind
your dresser, from the least space
between sneakers and shorts in your closet

that face, that goat-stink, that spiral
of horn—that woman hot on the tail
of bad spirits, whooping, was barely
more than you, Mikey, but with
the charge of you. *There!* I yanked
the windows closed and locked them
on the Rhine night air, on the
stagnant concrete postwar compound
where every family among us was in trouble,

ranked and quartered in a grid of buildings
and rooted to jetsam: calling cards,
cocktail parties, *Putzfrauen*, the best
at the PX duty-free. And the children's
illnesses growing less somatic with age,
the unkindest marriages lasting,
the drugs, black-marketing, drinking.

In Little America, I saw how lost
we were. I saw we'd brought nothing with us
there but goods. And there as well,
in my own kitchen, rigid as a mare
in a twitch, I saw for the first time
the word *dependent* pocket us, woman and child
together, where our feet couldn't reach
the ground. Had we been back in the air
over mid-Atlantic and the engines failing,
I, who freeze at the thought of open water,
could not have been less able to save you.

What you saw in my body that night
—and how many others, as our known world
shattered?—was my fingertip grip on you
and a piece of debris floating in that sea,
my instinct-wish to stand between you
and the terrors of which I was a part.
Remember our trip to the Wax Museum?
Remember the scene through the arched portcullis
into the Colosseum, the mother standing
on the soaked sand? Her hope put her there
in the first place, Mikey, in front
of the lions, put the boy, hip-tall, at her back.

Thirteen Next Birthday

(after losing the last custody fight)

~

Today, after school, in the bookshop door,
a boy your age waited for his mother.
You know the place. Bear Pond.
I watched as he sat on the steps, all knees
and elbows, in his first-month-of-school
uniform: blue *whoosh* on white sneakers,
new Levis a size too long, the strap
of a bookpack weighing his shoulder
where the fine skin of his neck rose up
to the jaw—its line just starting

to strengthen—a boy on the edge
of beginning a man, though his cheek,
its fragile balance of colors, painted him
still a child. All over town there must
have been a dozen beautiful doubles for him:
your eyes are brown, too. And your hair,
like his. And you would have left me
soon enough as it was. But now
what was ours to finish may never be done.
As love, I can but govern myself, hourly,
for your sake. Years now, your name
on any paper has not been mine, and nowhere
is what we are to each other our own:

the mother, the son. So your father
has claimed you. You've gone to learn
that a man may not be what a man uses,
that what a man loses, he owns.
I can see him invite you for the first time
high up, to where you may view this dominion:
below is all you are loved by, and love,
but his eyes are on you, his hand sweeps out
in an arc that describes your known, whole world—
even, between us, the paired birds purling
like one word for wisdom and power.

Bad Lay

~

You cut your baby teeth on
whores. Too young to drive,
you sat in the wife's seat
as your brother ferried you
down, over the border, the big
bill from your father folded
in his pocket. How terrible
for you, this first great
lie, the lie against which
you would measure every woman,
against which every woman
must fail: *rotten lay, boring
lay*, the mothers imbedded among
the students; the wives, *lousy lays*,
among the girls. Nor was it
simply the hard nulliparous
bodies, the awestruck, daughterly
lust. At forty you were still
able to say of the various brown-
skinned hookers that you'd taken
in the stalls of their poverty:
*They liked me. They said I was
really a man. They came.* If you

were not dangerous, armed,
as you are, with that wealth, with
the power the world strips

at the instant of birth from its
daughter, to bestow, with his own,
on the shoulders of its son, if your
very body were not a weapon that you
had raised against me, I could take you
into my arms and rock you, letting
my tears stream over your face
for the pain of your ignorance,
the silence money can buy.
Inside that silence is locked
the combination for that silence.
Thus the fruitlessness of love.
And we must part, leaving you
alone in the gray-green vault
of *your pleasure*, leaving me
in the red cauldron of my ire,
though it was together
that we made the mistake back then:
lovers thinking that I was your
student, lovers thinking
that you were my better.

Forty-five

~

All the others mothered up
and gone, it was my own

body's turn to be dandled,
instructed. So I watched,

in the ski lodge vanity
mirror, the woman cast like me

—compact, shapely—but
younger and dressed as never

I was, shake out her heavy
waist-length hair with her hand

from beneath, from the nape,
arching her body off to one side

or tossing forward her head
and the mane over. To it

she never touched a comb, but,
strand by strand, mindless

of time, back from its tangle
of play to a sheet of silk

released it. What I turned
back to in the mirror was

haste, usefulness, the face
of the woman in the market,

budget hair. And the years of
days it had taken her to grow

that virgin fall of auburn
that had been my shade.

Morning

for Terri Williams

~

Valentine has come in
after a whole August night
outdoors, her fur, her body
itself a tincture of the meadow
that borders the forest, of
the forest as well. I bend,
I fall to greet her. I smell
—all earth—the story of her
last dark hours awake out there alone.
She tells me everything. She keeps
nothing back for herself like
a person, afraid of loss.
And when I put the spoon down
into the bowl of cereal and milk,
she finds a place to sit and wait,
eye-level, for the bit she expects
me to leave her—who has just
returned with everything and
shared it with me, as the lesson
that joy deserves always more.

Mikey the Engineer: 1971

As if it were this very day—
it was this time of year, amber

October—I see you perched
in the first wagon, tugged

down the track of tune
before which I stand with the new

baby. Your yellow jumpsuit
matches his: you the new big boy.

And you see me see you chugging
round and round, your hair

the day's most golden thing,
a shy excitement poised

in your face like a present
hidden behind you. I understand

that you understand this is
practice in going away, the one

office a son and a mother
are given to perfect together.

Your face inches toward me
on the toy journey, full, then

three-fourths, starting past,
then your profile, a quarter,

gone. The back of your head
is a barbered nape. You do not turn.

I do not call. Today my heart
grieves twice, remembering

that day, when it first grieved.
When I first shamed it silent.

Le Coursier de Jeanne D'Arc

~

You know that they burned her horse
before her. Though it is not recorded,
you know that they burned her Percheron
first, before her eyes, because you

know that story, so old that story,
the routine story, carried to its
extreme, of the cruelty that can make
of what a woman hears *a silence,*

that can make of what a woman sees
a lie. She had no son for them to burn,
for them to take from her in the world
not of her making and put to its pyre,

so they layered a greater one in front of
where she was staked to her own—
as you have seen her pictured sometimes,
her eyes raised to the sky. But they were

not raised. This is yet one of their lies.
They were not closed. Though her hands
were bound behind her, and her feet were
bound deep in what would become fire,

she watched. Of greenwood stakes
head-high and thicker than a man's waist

they laced the narrow corral that would not
burn until flesh had burned, until

bone was burning, and laid it thick
with tinder—fatted wicks and sulphur,
kindling and logs—and ran a ramp
up to its height from where the gray horse

waited, his dapples making of his flesh
a living metal, layers of life
through which the light shone out
in places as it seems to through the flesh

of certain fish, a light she knew
as purest, coming, like that, from within.
Not flinching, not praying, she looked
the last time on the body she knew

better than the flesh of any man, or child,
or woman, having long since left the lap
of her mother—the chest with its
perfect plates of muscle, the neck

with its perfect, prow-like curve,
the hindquarters'—pistons—powerful cleft
pennoned with the silk of his tail.
Having ridden as they did together

—those places, that hard, that long—
their eyes found easiest that day
the way to each other, their bodies
wedded in a sacrament unmediated

by man. With fire they drove him
up the ramp and off into the pyre
and tossed the flame in with him.
This was the last chance they gave her

to recant her world, in which their power
came not from God. Unmoved, the Men
of God began watching him burn, and better,
watching her watch him burn, hearing

the long mad godlike trumpet of his terror,
his crashing in the wood, the groan
of stakes that held, the silverblack hide,
the pricked ears catching first

like dryest bark, and the eyes.
And she knew, by this agony, that she
might choose to live still, if she would
but make her sign on the parchment

they would lay before her, which now
would include this new truth: that it
did not happen, this death in the circle,
the rearing, plunging, raging, the splendid

armor-colored head raised one last time
above the flames before they took him
—like any game untended on the spit—into
their yellow-green, their blackening red.

Revision

~

Absorbed in the work, final touches
to a poem that rings true, she is stopped.
She lifts her head but does not turn to see
whose eyes are on her, have her in a locking
beam, the eyes of a tiger. She knows. It is
herself, the first time coming, a drink
in her hand, her face at midnight blotched
and swollen with crying. At the desk she sits
erect to let the other see her.
The house around the two of them is order
and light and quiet. The writer faces
a window, and from outside, snow and
the light on it, backlight her shape,
silhouette it, making of a woman typing
a page a faceless, mythic figure. Then,
she was the two of them, as she is now,
and she sits a long time still to be
apprehended, deeply, her happiness
in the small—her own—that surrounds her.
And she leans unsteady on the doorframe
appraising the woman at abysmal distance
as a longing streams between them across
the room of years, a tenderness exchanged
in the common body.

The Mother Chooses Divorce in Her Fifty-third Year

~

For room and board, says
the great man. *For those
vacations. For the clothes
you wore.* Her heart says,

*You were in prison all
those years. You were doing
time,* when she asks what
she worked for. She leaves

anyway, with a new suit,
pocket cash. An angry woman
is already in the wrong. A mother
angry is a woman to be hushed,

frightening as a priest angry
bearing the gold ciborium. Still,
if a street gang left you
senseless, but alive, as they

jostled off with chest-checks
after the boots and chains,
what you would wake to first—
your death pressing into

your cheek like gravel—
would be gratitude. To have been
strong and practical as a
well-made tool. To have

been made of know-how,
a root cellar of wisdoms,
daily, hourly. How terrible,
for nothing. The years

passed like calendar pages
in a movie. Confessor,
nurse. Chef de cuisine.
She thinks in these terms,

air traffic control.
A donkey pulling a cart.
A piece—twice a day in the
twice-a-day years—a cart

following a donkey. To have
been beautiful, and beautiful
for a long time and not
to have gotten hard cash of it.

That beauty thinned with the
thinning of illusion, the hope
time would lead to love. How
terrible what it taught them

—about love—who were the
factory she labored in, woke to,
slept in after the last was
asleep, like a fireman in his

clothes. Now they were
abroad, conceived in ignorance,
the boys, the girls.
But with the lightest heart

in memory she steps out,
stripped as a woman 30 years
in a coma, but carrying only
her own weight, the one cup,

which feeling, not having known it
before, and not able to see it
mock her fallen face,
she confuses with youth.

At Holy Family Church

~

Sunday morning, and we kneel
as one in the usual pew: my mother
with her hat's veil drawn down
over pancake and bruises,
my father soldered into his iron
suit of hangover and rage, my brother
—live fiber of terror—riveted
to the closest exit: to become
the man in skirts and power lifting
the gold ciborium. I hold
my whole body like a single breath
—nowhere is open—and to
the side altar's lifesize family say
the oldest prayer, for my own.
Of plaster, of soft pastels, warm
ochres—loved eyes, loved hair—
of gold, of the peaceful plumb
of their garments, of hands
that are open, their circle is made,
and every gesture is a form of touch
for which I can learn a name. *Mother,
Father,* even the sandalled feet
that stem them to earth seem molded
to a purpose: the quiet in which
the child my age stands barefoot.
That is one world, my voice says to me,
and this is another. How far must I

walk or swim or fly? I am nobody's
child from then. I am some child's
mother, laying a heart torn from its nave
between that morning and that time.

The Apple Tree

for my mother

~

More beautiful now than ever you were
in pale May blossom, or in August,
gravid again—your chained boughs
bearing, your skirts, stiff camouflage
arustle—you stand, past use, past
prettiness in the winter of your winter,
at the brink of encroaching woods, in the yard
of the old farm, where now, out windows,
curtains shake themselves like rags
from a lost cleaning morning. Here,
in the light that by noon takes
your shadow and carries it from the garden
to the barn, now, from your deep
seeking source under snow, drink long,
breathe slow, be still, as did the child,
she of the single body. The many that
found you and took you are fallen away.